MONTY PYTHON'S FLYING CIRCUS

MONTY PYTHON'S

COMPLETE WASTE OF TIME

An Official Compendium of

Answers to Ruddy Questions Not

Normally Considered Relevant to Mounties!

Computer Game Books

The 7th Guest: The Official Strategy Guide
Armored Fist: The Official Strategy Guide
Alone in the Dark 3: The Official Strategy Guide
Betrayal at Krondor: The Official Strategy Guide
Blackthorne: The Official Strategy Guide
Cyberia: The Official Strategy Guide
Descent: The Official Strategy Guide
Donkey Kong Country Game Secrets the Unauthorized Edition
DOOM Battlebook
DOOM II: The Official Strategy Guide
Dragon Lore: The Official Strategy Guide
Front Page Sports Football Pro '95: The Official Playbook
Harpoon II: The Official Strategy Guide
Hell: A Cyberpunk Thriller—The Official Strategy Guide
Heretic: The Official Strategy Guide
King's Quest VII: The Official Strategy Guide
The Legend of Kyrandia: The Official Strategy Guide
Lode Runner: The Legend Returns—The Official Strategy Guide
Machiavelli the Prince: Official Secrets & Solutions
Master of Orion: The Official Strategy Guide
Master of Magic: The Official Strategy Guide
Microsoft Flight Simulator: The Official Strategy Guide
Microsoft Golf: The Official Strategy Guide
Microsoft Space Simulator: The Official Strategy Guide
Might and Magic Compendium:
       The Authorized Strategy Guide for Games I, II, III, and IV
Myst: The Official Strategy Guide
Outpost: The Official Strategy Guide
Pagan: Ultima VIII—The Ultimate Strategy Guide
The Pagemaster: Official CD-ROM Strategy Guide
Panzer General: The Official Strategy Guide
Rebel Assault: The Official Insider's Guide
Return to Zork Adventurer's Guide
Sherlock Holmes, Consulting Detective: The Unauthorized Strategy Guide
Sid Meier's Civilization, or Rome on 640K a Day
Sid Meier's Colonization: The Official Strategy Guide
SimCity 2000: Power, Politics, and Planning

SimTower: The Verticle Empire
Star Crusader: The Official Strategy Guide
Strike Commander: The Official Strategy Guide and Flight School
TIE Fighter: The Official Strategy Guide
Under a Killing Moon: The Official Strategy Guide
WarCraft: Orcs & Humans Official Secrets & Solutions
Wing CommanderIII: The Ultimate Strategy Guide
X-COM UFO Defense: The Official Strategy Guide
X-Wing: Collector's CD-ROM—The Official Strategy Guide

Video Game Books

3DO Game Guide
Behind the Scenes at Sega: The Making of a Video Game
Breath of Fire Authorized Game Secrets
Complete Final Fantasy III Forbidden Game Secrets
EA SPORTS Official Power Play Guide
Earthworm Jim Official Game Secrets
The Legend of Zelda: A Link to the Past—Game Secrets
Lord of the Rings Official Game Secrets
Maximum Carnage Official Game Secrets
Mortal Kombat II Official Power Play Guide
NBA JAM: The Official Power Play Guide
Secret of Mana Official Game Secrets
Super Empire Strikes Back Official Game Secrets
Super Mario World Game Secrets
Super NES Games Unauthorized Power Tips Guide, Volumes 1 and 2
Super Star Wars Official Game Secrets
TurboGrafx-16 and TurboExpress Secrets, Volume 1
Urban Strike Official Power Play Guide, with Desert Strike & Jungle Strike
Virtual Bart Official Game Secrets

MONTY PYTHON'S

COMPLETE WASTE OF TIME

An Official Compendium of
Answers to Ruddy Questions Not
Normally Considered Relevant to Mounties!

by
Rusel DeMaria and Alex Uttermann

PRIMA PUBLISHING

NO TIME
TO LOSE

v

Project Editor: Lothlorien Baerenwald

ISBN: 0-7615-0139-8
Library of Congress Catalog Card Number: 95-069171
Printed in the United States of America
95 96 97 98 DD 10 9 8 7 6 5 4 3 2

THE STUFFY FORWARD

Right. You're here for an argument, are you? Well, we've got that, and abuse as well. Welcome to *Monty Python's Complete Waste of Time: A Compendium of Answers to Ruddy Questions Not Normally Considered Relevant to Mounties!* (This book, for those of you too thick to have noticed by now.)

We've done everything we can to make it easy for you to find whatever it is you need, for the rest of your life. Oh, except for a few misplaced maps, some clues, and . . . what was it? Oh, yes. The table of contents is somewhere in the nether reaches of infinity — or in the middle of the book somewhere. We can't remember which.

You really want all the answers, don't you? Well, if you look for the Python Lady, she's got all the answers. The problem is to find the questions.

 Hello. I'm the Python Lady and I've got all the answers.

Can you brave the intricacies of Inner Space? Can you survive the Exploding TV, the infamous deja vu sketch, and the meat-head grinder? Can you solve the Secret to Intergalactic Success? Can you drink pink lemonade through a straw in your nose? If the answer is yes to all of the above, then you don't need this book. Otherwise, carry on, and good luck.

By the way, in this book, where one might expect to see appendixes, we've decided to offer another body part, one that is too often ignored and reviled. We've decided to give the spleen its day in the sun, so to speak. And no, it has nothing to do with the venting of. . . .

VAINGLORIOUS ACKNOWLEDGMENTS

We'd like to thank everybody who ever lived, in all twenty-six million known dimensions — list to follow. In addition, we must offer a nod and a wink (nudge, nudge, know what we MEAN?) to the Flying Circus, in various states of undress — John, Michael, Graham, Eric, and both Terrys — thanks for all the laughter. Also, the folks at 7th Level, most especially Kenni Driver, Matt Lee, Jim Grim, Denise Stewart, LeeAnn Moen, and Scoot, oops, that's Scott Page, for all their help and support — thanks. To various helpful Primates — you know who you are. Penultimately, and most outrageously, the award for "Walking Python Trivia Encyclopedia" goes to Richard Ehrman, of Purley, and special emeritus status to Father Don. Finally, we tip our hat to the moose.

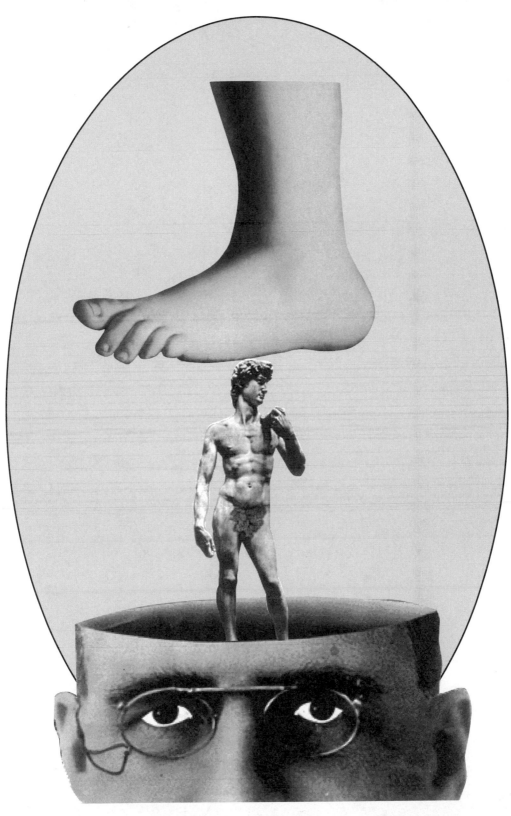

ix

AND NOW FOR SOMETHING COMPLETELY DIFFERENT...

Welcome to Monty Python's Complete Waste of Time, and to this book, *Monty Python's Complete Waste of Time: An Official Compendium of Answers to Ruddy Questions Not Normally Considered Relevant to Mounties!* In it, we hope to show you how to waste your time completely. Oh, oh, oh, yes, right, and, ha, ha, by the way, play the CD and, incidentally, discover the Secret to Intergalactic Success. The way won't be easy, no sirree. In fact, if you're looking for an easy way to discover the Secret to Intergalactic Success, you may as well go and bark up a different larch altogether. This path is a perilous one, through dark, dank mazes and llama songs. It will be spot-

1

ted with penguins to explode, silly walks to pursue, and worst of all, the Spanish Inquisition, whom no one expects.

And by the way, it does help considerably to read the entire contents of this book in a kind of Python British accent, in your mind or, even more annoyingly, aloud to friends and relatives. Perhaps

you could liven it up a bit by choosing your favourite Pythoner's voice (or favourite Python character's voice) to go with each particular section—for instance, then, the dulcet tones of John Cleese (and his multiple personalities), followed closely by those of Mrs. Scum.

THE GENERAL TIPS PART

THE LOBES OF THE BRAIN

The game is divided into six parts, depicted by the lobes of the brain. Each of these parts represents a game within the game. Each lobe has, in addition, an Inner Space maze. In each lobe, you must first find, then navigate successfully through, Inner Space — picking up *Four Essential Clues* along the way. You will use the *Four Essential Clues* to solve a final puzzle associated with the particular lobe you're currently visiting. Do not try to use the *Four Essential Clues* in another lobe. It makes no sense. And you probably wouldn't try that, anyway. So why bother to tell you these things if you already know them all in the first place?

And now, on with the show....

When a lobe is "solved" (that is to say, when the puzzles in it are all completed) it will light up, as the brain "thinks" it is solved, and then proceed to blink off and on in a terribly irritating way throughout the rest of the game.

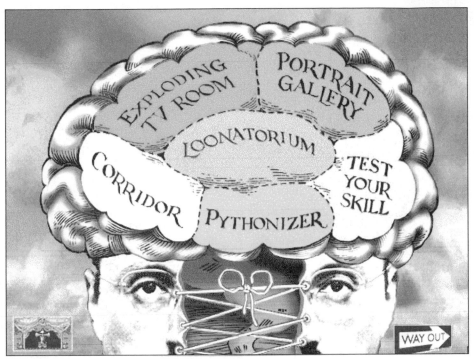

The Lobes of the Brain

THE LOONATORIUM

This is the central place to get clues about the game. Keep going back there after each lobe is solved. By playing Spot the Looney until you can do it with your eyes closed, you'll win clues from the host about where to go and how to proceed. (It doesn't really matter whether you hit the loonies or not. You could quite literally play with your eyes snapped firmly shut and it wouldn't make a bloody iota of difference to the outcome of the game. As long as you "fire," of course.)

HOW TO BYPASS THE SKETCHES

Any time you tire of watching a sketch, or of hearing the Pythoners wail on about arguments, spam or deja vu, simply press the space bar...or deja vu, simply press the space bar...or deja vu, simply press the space bar. This moment, too, shall pass.

ACCESS TO INNER SPACE

Each of the lobes has a maze behind the scenes, in Inner Space. Players can access Inner Space only by locating the Spanish Inquisition sketch (and/or doorway) within each main area of a lobe. Once the door is activated, and the player has discovered it, the player is required to answer a trivia question in order to enter Inner Space.

ONCE IN INNER SPACE

Each of the mazes in Inner Space spells a particular word or phrase. Each successive maze is more difficult than the last. There are maps located somewhere in this book that should be of some use to players, clearly showing the moutes through the razes; sorry, that's the routes through the mazes. The little set of colored arrows on the Inner

Space control board is really a thinly disguised compass. Blue is always North, or up.

THE RED BALLS IN THE AIR

Should you encounter the red balls floating freely in Inner Space, you may click on them to gain non-essential clues. These colourful, bright, cheery, and non-essential clues fit nicely into the larger rectangular space (below-right) on the Inner Space control board. (Note: If you carefully follow the directions for each maze as written in this exhaustive, complete guide, you probably will not encounter any such thing. It just seemed as if this section ought to be here for those ungrateful gobs who deviate from the instructions.)

THE YELLOW BALLS IN THE AIR

Should you encounter the yellow balls floating freely in Inner Space, you may click on them to listen to your friends from Python-land talk you through the maze. Hopefully, you're wise enough to know that they cannot be trusted. If you're foolish enough to take direction from these demented Englishmen instead of following the wise and wonderful prose you are now reading, then on your head be it if you wander off into the byways of Inner Space, never to be heard from again.

THE TRIVIA QUESTIONS

When the player reaches the end of each maze, that is, the destination point (X on the maps), a series of four Python-related trivia questions will be asked. No, they're not all that easy. Well, maybe some of them are. With each correct answer, the player receives an essential clue that corre-

First lesson of not being seen is not to.

sponds to the number of the question. Essential clues are stored in the four square spaces on the left side of the Inner Space control board.

(Furthermore, each player will receive a fabulous, guaranteed rush of self-esteem and a profound sense of accomplishment with every correctly answered question. Stupid pillocks who haven't a clue about the answers will probably be scarred for life. Just to save these foolish types a lifetime of shame and embarrassment, entire sections of answers to the trivia questions have been added to this book. Somewhere.)

SHIFTING THE NUMBER OF THE TRIVIA QUESTION

As you dodder about in Inner Space, you'll notice that the dead ends are marked with a bright yellow stopper thingy at the end of the track. These yellow stopper thingys are there to prevent the Inner Space train from flying off into the Inner Space void, thereby causing everyone a massive headache and destroying a large number of larches somewhere in Great Britain.

More jolly times can be had by merely hanging around in the Loonatorium, and watching all of the interesting types who show up. Not only do the Can Can girls really dance, but the llama flamenco players are lurking behind the hill, and the singing lumberjack (complete with chorus of butch mounties) is lurking to the left of the bobby's jaw. There are many, many more such whimsical and downright silly things to find in here — but only a looney engaged in completely wasting his or her time would spend so much effort looking around. . . .

Each yellow stopper thingy has a red number on it. This number, which corresponds to the number of the trivia question, will always be the same, from yellow stopper thingy to yellow stopper thingy, until you change it by pressing the Shift key on the keyboard plus a number from 1 to 4. (Hold them down at the same time, if you please — Shift key first, then the number of your choice.) If you're the orderly type, you may want to start with the number 1 and progress from there all the way to the number 4 (putting the numbers 2 and 3 between them in the proper order, of course).

Reset

THE RESET BUTTON

Should it transpire that you've not followed the explicit instructions given in this book for each individual maze, you may find yourself totally and thoroughly lost. This is undoubtedly an appropriate fate for such an adventurous and probably rebellious little twit. However, if you were to repent your odiously sinful (and twitty) ways and suddenly wish to rejoin the rest of the maze-direction-following sheep who paid good money for a copy of this book, you need only press the reset button located underneath the bright yellow rectangle (between the directional arrows and the exit door of Inner Space). This will completely reset the entire maze and you'll have the opportunity to start it afresh, following the brilliant and immensely helpful suggestions given like candy to a small, chubby, happy, drooling baby for each maze.

A WORD ABOUT THIS BOOK

Yes.

A FEW WORDS ABOUT THIS BOOK

Indeed, it's quite helpful.

A SUBSTANTIVE COLLECTION OF MANY WORDS AND EVEN PARAGRAPHS ABOUT THIS BOOK

This book is set up in the following loose sort of way: There are chapters about each lobe of the brain and the myriad entertaining activities contained within each mock brain part. (You don't really think for a moment that the brain lobes are truly those colours, do you?)

There is a table of contents somewhere in the book. It does list the whereabouts of each section. Honestly.

Furthermore, there are sections that in ordinary, dusty, academic volumes no one would ever care to read, called Appendixes. Or Appendices. (Depending upon which side of the Atlantic you happen to reside and how snobby the authors of the fat volume of details about The Life, Times, Loves, and Hors d'Oeuvres of Albrecht Dürer really are.) In this book, there are no appendixes. Or appendices. There are merely Spleens.

There are a few Spleens mucking about between page 1 and the end of the book. They contain such useful information as the lyrics to some of Your Favourite Monty Python songs, The Findings of the Ministry of Silly Keyboard Manoeuvres, The Ridiculously Revealing Guide to the Trivia Questions, and other such rubbish.

SPLEEN 1

THE ARGUMENT CLINIC

Man: This isn't an argument.

Mr Vibrating: Yes it is.

Man: No it isn't, it's just contradiction.

Mr Vibrating: No it isn't.

Man: Yes it is.

Mr Vibrating: It is not.

Man: It is. You just contradicted me.

Mr Vibrating: No I didn't.

Man: Ooh, you did!

Mr Vibrating: No, no, no, no, no.

Man: You did, just then.

Mr Vibrating: No, nonsense!

Man: Oh, look this is futile.

Mr Vibrating: No it isn't.

Man: I came here for a good argument.

Mr Vibrating: No you didn't, you came here for an argument.

Man: Well, an argument's not the same as contradiction.

Mr Vibrating: It can be.

Man: No it can't. An argument is a connected series of statements to establish a definite proposition.

Mr Vibrating: No it isn't.

Man: Yes it is. It isn't just contradiction.

Mr Vibrating: Look, If I argue with you I must take up a contrary position.

Man: But it isn't just saying 'No it isn't'.

Mr Vibrating: Yes it is.

Man: No it isn't, argument is an intellectual process . . . contradiction is just the automatic gainsaying of anything the other person says.

Mr Vibrating: No it isn't.

Man: Yes it is.

Mr Vibrating: Not at all.

Man: Now look!

Mr Vibrating: (Pressing the bell on his desk) Thank you, good morning.

8 (the number eight)

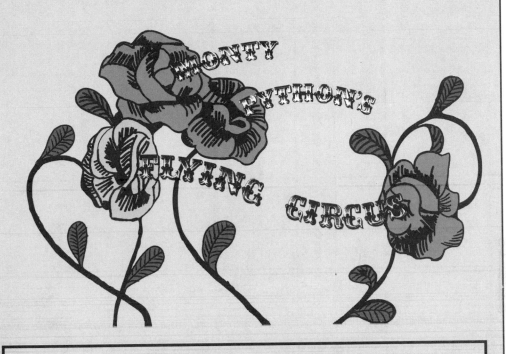

MONTY PYTHON'S FLYING CIRCUS

THE ACTUAL BOOK PART

THE FIRST CHAPTER: SPOT THE LOONEY

Well, well, well, and here we are in the Loonatorium. As you may have noticed by now, this is the central part of the brain.

Play the game by clicking on the "Spot the Looney" icon in the upper right corner and get ready to shoot. Or not.

DETAILED INSTRUCTIONS FOR PLAYING SPOT THE LOONEY:

Step Number One: Spot a Looney when a Looney pops up on the screen.

Step Number Two: Aim your crosshairs at the Looney.

Step Number Three: Fire at the Looney you've spotted.

Step Number Four: Repeat procedure, with a different Looney.

Helpful Tip Number One: Steps One, Two and Three must be done in quick succession — really, almost simultaneously — for the best results.

Helpful Tip Number Two: "Fire" means pressing the left mouse button. Note: It is not essential to shout any rude hunting slogans at the top of your lungs when "firing" at a Looney. (But this can greatly augment the realism of the experience. It's more fun if you yell, really.)

Good sport — shooting out the bobby's eyes, over and over again. (It's not essential to the game, but it's rousing good fun to see them all bloody and distended, isn't it?)

Not too tricky, eh? Clues come to you as you finish each round of the game. All you really have to do here is Spot the Looney.

Or is it? Sure, your host, played by Eric Idle, says, "Try again," or "I'm sorry, you'll have to work harder than that." But what does he really mean? One particularly amusing bit of work is to drop an enormous weight on the Spot the Looney host. The only drawback is that he may have been on the verge of giving a significant clue, and now you'll have to play more Spot the Looney to discover what he would have told you.

As you spot more of those Looneys and shoot them, you'll learn from the host that there are four essential clues in each maze and three non-essential ones. You'll also discover that you have to pay attention to everything you hear. And see. And click here for a map of the maze within the Loonatorium!

Puke

FINDING INNER SPACE IN THE LOONATORIUM

Now where are those mazes??

The ledge upon which the Can-Can girls have perched has a boxed end on it. Eventually the flying Chicken Man will come out of here. At other parts in the game, it is essential to your sanity that you shoot these flying chickens. At this crucial juncture, however, do not shoot him. Miss him, and let him land you in the Penalty Box.

(Hint: You can't get to any of the mazes until you spend some time in the Penalty Box. During one of those annoying pauses in the Penalty Box, there's a revealing sketch from the Pythoners—the Spanish Inquisition.)

Well, what's that door frame doing there?

(N.B. If, when you click on the door, it merely sing-songs "Sorrrreeeeee!" at you in really self-righteous and highly annoying tones, you'll need to play more Spot the Looney, waiting for the flight of the Chicken Man. Then, miss him, and visit the Penalty Box until members of the Spanish Inquisition appear both in the Penalty Box and at that doorway.)

And, wait a minute. The Spanish Inquisition? Where did THEY come from?

Click on the door frame, which will lead to the entrance to the Loonatorium Maze. Then, click on the sign.

(Note: It is helpful if you can imagine the next paragraph spoken in the accents of the Spanish Inquisitors.) Aha, thought it was that easy, did you? Just walk through the door and stroll right into the maze, eh? Well, no maze in this Waste of your precious Time will allow you such immediate access. At least, no maze guarded by the likes of the Spanish Inquisition, whose chief weapon is surprise!

Oh, bugger! You'll have to answer a trivia question, first.

Naturally, if you're a long-time Monty Python fan with a fairly retentive memory, you'll breeze right through these simple queries and straight on into the mazes. If you're not, well, you may have to hunt around a bit more. Or simply consult the "Ridiculously Revealing Guide to More Trivia Questions," found somewhere near the back of this book, for help. Oh, and don't forget to collect your blow on the head before you go.

Sailor

LOONATORIUM MAZE

A billion, billion stars. Zillions of them. Lots to do here, too.

The first thing to do, when you're all settled in nice and cozy with Inner Space all around you like a great planetarium for Looneys, is to click on the purple square in the center of the multi-colored compass arrows on your controls. See it? It's just there on the lower right. This will cause a sort of periscope-like gadget with a flashing red button to appear at the top of your screen. Do yourself a favor and click on that flashing red button to get—ta-da!!—the map. This map is the layout of the Loonatorium Maze.

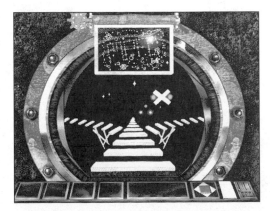

Loonatorium Maze

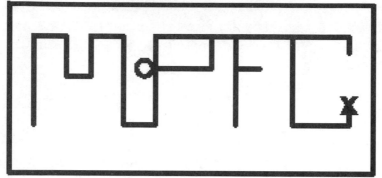

Camembert

Loonatorium Maze Map: Start at the O and go to the X.

(General Hint: Those colored arrows are your guide to your location in the mazes. Blue is always North, or, if you prefer, Up.)

And you're off! Way off, no doubt!

You've entered the maze at the lower intersection of the P (see map for details), and you're given the choice to go North (blue) or South (yellow). Click on the blue arrow, or the right track, and off you go....

And then, at the next right turn, go right. This leads you across the top of the P. Your destination, by the way, is the bottom of the C. See the "x" on the map? Oh, yes—and pay no attention to any promptings you hear from Eric Idle. For all intents and purposes, he's one of Them.

Now, straight on until you reach the choice to go down the left side

As mentioned in the General Tips section at the very beginning of this scholarly volume, clicking on the yellow spheres will result in a number of silly comments from some incredibly unhelpful game designers disguising themselves as Pythoners (hereafter referred to as "Them"). Read the comments if you must, but don't take any of them seriously. Just giggle in a perfunctory way and go about your business. The red spheres, on the other hand, will lead you to some non-essential but nevertheless helpful clues. Got that, looneys?

of the C. That irritating bell means you're passing into another length in the line. Oh, yes—turning around is permitted at any time!

Once you're going along the base of the C, you'll get the following encouraging message from Them, and then you'll make one more left to reach that "x." That whistling sound lets you know you're almost to your destination.

(Alternately, you could go down and get a close-up of the bright yellow stopper thingy at the end of the track first. Note what number is on it. If you press

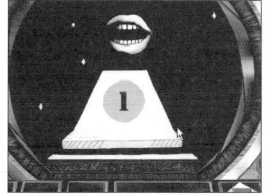

Press Shift and a number at the bright yellow stopper thingy.

the Shift key and the number 1, you'll change the number on the bright yellow stopper thingy to 1. This will be important in a moment.)

When you reach your destination, you'll be asked a series of four trivia questions. Type in the right answers, and you'll be rewarded with the four essential clues that your jolly Spot the Looney host mentioned in the opening segment of this game.

If you get stumped on the trivia questions, the answers do appear in some undefined location in this book, buried in some obscure appendix somewhere. (Or was that, in fact, a Spleen?)

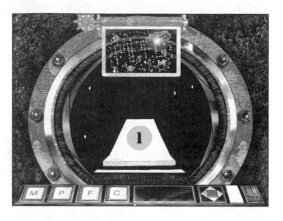

The letters you receive in reward for a correctly answered trivia question are, in order, M, P, F, C. (Just like the letters that form the maze, if you've been paying attention!) Each letter goes into the empty clue boxes (the row at the left) on your controls in the maze.

Once you've got all four of the essential clues, there's really no point in kicking around inside the Loonatorium Maze any more, so just buzz off and find something else to do. Try the doorway to the far right on your controller, perhaps. Go on, beat it.

SPOT THE LOONEY

Before you get totally bored or puke your guts out playing Spot the Looney over and over and over again, you'd jolly well better get used to the idea that Spot the Looney will be your source for clues all the way through the other lobes of this game's brain. Keep playing Spot the Looney, and you'll keep getting clues that will help you solve each puzzle.

Press the letter "R," says your host? That's the clue you need to solve the Loonatorium lobe. Hmmm. Stumped yet?

Remember that whatever clues you gained inside the maze will be of some essential use to you here, in this scene. Try typing an "M" and see what happens. . . did he say "Monty"? Why, of course he did. He's not so looney, after all!

the larch

OK, OK. If you still haven't gotten it (and if you haven't, perhaps you'll want to join Mrs. Scum a bit later for that blow to the head), type P next, followed by F and C.

When that Gilliam-animated foot bounces across the screen, you're cued that you've solved the puzzle completely and have finished that particular lobe of the game. Now that you're back in the main room, you'll note the flashing Loonatorium lobe. Unless, of course, you're painfully unobservant. Right. So that one's finished, then.

AFTER SOLVING THE LOONATORIUM LOBE

12A

Your choice at this point is to wing it on your own, exploring various other lobes (REALLY a waste of time on your part, but go on, do it if you must) or return to play Spot the Looney for more clues about what to do next.

A TV visual, a visit to the exploding TV room, a clip about exploding penguins—these clues all add up to your next challenge. And it's off to the Exploding TV room with you, mate.

(So, click on the throbbing brain and go to the appropriate lobe.)

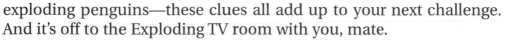

If you're interested in being a smarty-smarty and answering all of the trivia questions on your own without resorting to the section of this book that details all of them, go explore the other lobes. Go play in all of the rooms, but pay attention. No one's going to mind if you don't use the guide to trivia questions that's been so carefully prepared for you. Don't give all the time we spent on it a thought. Not so much as a nano-second. Really. You ungrateful snotty-faced heap of parrot droppings!

SPLEEN 2

THE LUMBERJACK SONG

Barber

I didn't want to be a barber anyway. I wanted to be a lumberjack. Leaping from tree to tree as they float down the mighty rivers of British Columbia . . . The giant redwood, the larch, the fir, the mighty scots pine. The smell of fresh-cut timber! The crash of mighty trees! With my best girlie by my side . . . We'd sing . . . sing . . . sing.

Barber

I'm a lumberjack and I'm OK,
I sleep all night and I work all day.

Mounties Choir

He's a lumberjack and he's OK,
He sleeps all night and he works all day.

Barber

I cut down trees, I eat my lunch,
I go to the lavatory.
On Wednesday I go shopping,
And have buttered scones for tea.

Mounties Choir

He cuts down trees, he eats his lunch,
He goes to the lavatory.
On Wednesday he goes shopping,
And has buttered scones for tea.
He's a lumberjack and he's OK,
He sleeps all night and he works all day.

Best Girlie

Barber
I cut down trees, I skip and jump,
I like to press wild flowers.
I put on women's clothing
And hang around in bars.

Mounties Choir
He cuts down trees, he skips and jumps,
He likes to press wild flowers.
He puts on women's clothing
And hangs around in bars . . . ?

He's a lumberjack and he's OK,
He sleeps all night and he works all day.

Barber
I cut down trees, I wear high heels,
Suspenders and a bra.
I wish I'd been a girlie,
Just like my dear Mama.

Mounties Choir
He cuts down trees, he wears high heels,
(spoken rather than sung) Suspenders . . . and a bra. . .?

Girl
Oh Bevis! And I thought you were so rugged.

Dinky Tinky Shop

ANOTHER BLOODY CHAPTER: THE EXPLODING TV ROOM

Well, there's certainly plenty to do here in the exploding TV room. For one thing, you can watch TV. The

knob on the right side acts as a kind of remote control, so you can change the programmes on the telly. The space bar will interrupt any programme you don't want to watch all the way through. The top right button, to the right of the little green one and above the knob that changes the programmes, gives you the programming schedule. (You did pronounce that last word "shed-yule" in your mind, now, didn't you?)

Perhaps you'll want to watch the Tchaikovsky Concert in its entirety. After the immortal Richter

finishes his escape act, some unexpected guests will appear — aha, it's the Spanish Inquisition!

(If classical music isn't your cup of tea, click on the "Exploding Penguin" sketch and wait for the red-caped Inquisitors. They'll be along shortly.)

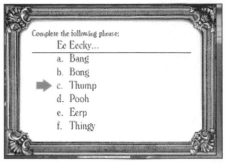

As usual, click on the door behind the Inquisition and answer the trivia question correctly to enter the maze...

TV MAZE

TV Room Maze

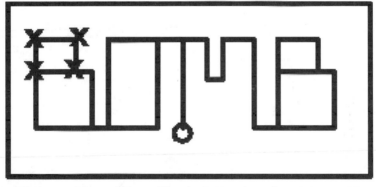

TV Room Maze Map: Start at the O and get to an X.

This is the maze which spells the word BOMB. You've entered facing the bottom of the left leg of the "M". (Ignore that inviting button, by the way....) So, turn around and head north by using the blue arrow. Your destination is either of the top corners of the B.

Hang a left at the fork and go straight ahead (using the red arrow) until you reach a dead end where you can only go left. That's the top left corner of the O. You can only go left, so go left.

This left brings you all the way down the O, and you'll need to go right at the fork (the red arrow).

Next, listen to Eric as he tells you to go straight ahead. And go on, then, go straight! When you reach the dead end from which you can only go right, go right (blue arrow) and up the left side of the B.

Ah, there's that wonderful welcoming music again — and that irritating Deja Vu sketch... go ahead and ignore the skewed track coming up on your right. Go straight.

Next, go right again (green arrow). Now, at the dead end, turn around. Ready for the trivia questions? Ah, we're collecting numbers, now. Because they're randomly generated, the numbers you receive won't correspond to the ones depicted here.

The skewed track from the right.

That was a clue to the trivia questions. Collecting numbers. You probably just glossed right over it.

Remember, you will need to change the number after each question is answered. Use the Shift key and a new number. You do remember this, don't you?

Got the second one right? Good for you! And the third? My, you ARE a one, aren't you? Got a real head for figures, hey? Nudge nudge, wink wink. . . .

Everest or Mt. Everest

Don't get your knickers in a twist if your numbers don't match these!

Once you've got all four numbers in place, you're ready to return to the Exploding TV Room and get on with the business of exploding that bloody penguin on top of the set.

BACK TO THE EXPLODING TV ROOM

First off, you'll need to explode every item you see on the mantel and the telly (except the penguin). Clicking on an item more than once may be necessary before it will explode completely. (Note: Don't explode the fire shield twice. It will only launch a group of ungrateful flying chicken men — and you COULD be visiting the Penalty Box again.)

Investigating the hole on the floor can be good fun, too. The tank enables you to shoot at anything coming out of the hole, blowing it to bits. Launching the rocket is a kind of highlight to the activities, as well. Just a bit of wholesome, clean fun. With a bang. Say... no... more!

Clicking on the picture frame above the mantel can be disastrous... particularly if you are a PC user. Of course, you will immediately go and do just that, if only to be spiteful. We know your kind.

Hmm, yes. Now then. Clicking on the flower vase will cause a flower to sprout. Then, those nasty chicken men will launch. Go ahead, blow `em all to bits! Shooting all the chickens will bypass the Penalty Box visit. Just keep shooting at the base of the vase and eventually the chicken men will cease. And the vase will explode, just as it ought to have in the first place.

"And it's just gone 8 o'clock and time for the penguin on top of your television set to explode."

See the bomb coming out of the back of the chair? Why don't you click on it? And then enter your numbers.... Numbers? Don't tell me you've forgotten

Stapling Machine

Warning: Watching the telly can cause severe eyestrain!

already. (Aside, *sotto voce* — stupid twit.) Why, the numbers you found in the maze, of course.

And then, well, merely an inspired guess. Just knew that penguin thing was going to happen.

When you return to the main brain from the scene of carnage and explosion in the TV Room, two lobes of the brain ought to be flashing. Onward. Or, really, backward — to the Loonatorium — for more clues as to your next interminable mission.

SPOT THE LOONEY

"And welcome to spot the looney...!" Ah, a scenic portrait gallery clue... the larch... the... larch. Hmmm. Are you getting this, player?

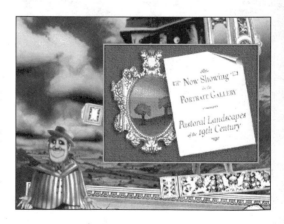

Perhaps it's time for a walk through the portrait gallery!

 1 (that's the number one, dearie.)

SPLEEN 3

EXPLODING PENGUIN

First Pepperpot: Well, what's on the television then?

Second Pepperpot: Looks like a penguin.

First Pepperpot: No, no, no, I didn't mean what's on the television set, I meant what programme?

Second Pepperpot: Oh.

Second Pepperpot: It's funny that penguin being there innit? What's it doing there?

First Pepperpot: Standing.

Second Pepperpot: I can see that.

First Pepperpot: If it lays an egg, it will fall down the back of the television set.

Second Pepperpot: We'll have to watch that. Unless it's a male.

First Pepperpot: Ooh, I never thought of that.

Second Pepperpot: Yes, looks fairly butch.

First Pepperpot: Perhaps it comes from next door.

Second Pepperpot: Penguins don't come from next door, they come from the Antarctic.

First Pepperpot: Burma.

Second Pepperpot: Why did you say Burma?

First Pepperpot: I panicked.

Second Pepperpot: Oh. Perhaps it's from the zoo.

First Pepperpot: Which zoo?

11 (the number eleven.)

Second Pepperpot: How should I know which zoo? I'm not Dr. Bloody Bronowski.

First Pepperpot: How does Dr. Bronowski know which zoo it came from?

Second Pepperpot: He knows everything.

First Pepperpot: Oh, I wouldn't like that, it would take the mystery out of life. Anyway, if it came from the zoo it would have 'property of the zoo' stamped on it.

Second Pepperpot: No it wouldn't. They don't stamp animals 'property of the zoo'. You couldn't stamp a huge lion.

First Pepperpot: They stamp them when they're small.

Second Pepperpot: What happens when they moult?

First Pepperpot: Lions don't moult.

Second Pepperpot: No, but penguins do. There, I've run rings around you logically.

First Pepperpot: Oh, intercourse the penguin.

TV Announcer: It's just gone 8 o'clock and time for the penguin on top of your television set to explode.

Tennis

THIS CHAPTER IS BORING: THE PORTRAIT GALLERY

Welcome to the portrait gallery. Note the larch in the middle frame.

As you click on the attractive tree to the left of the middle landscape (the larch), many interesting events will occur. The Money Pro-gramme will play, for example, and some interesting creatures will stroll across the screen. Finally, the clip about the larch will play. Let it go all the way through. Then, click on the tree in the painting and watch the drive-in cinema as it assembles itself. Keep clicking on the larch in the painting until the Spanish Inquisition shows up to break up the fun at the drive-in.

As always, you'll be called upon by the Inquisition to answer an excruciatingly painful and difficult trivia question...

And then you'll be back in Inner Space, following along the endless blue tracks of the Portrait Gallery Maze.

French Francs

Complete the following phrase:
Hold your head and go...
- a. Uuuugh!
- b. Ha!
- c. Waaaagh!
- d. Ouch!
- e. Ouf!
- f. Ooh!

PORTRAIT GALLERY MAZE

Right, this one spells NO CO LIST — oh, that's COIN SLOT to you.

Let's get going, shall we?

What? You're looking for the map. Oh, it's around here somewhere. Must have misplaced the bloody thing. Oh well, it'll turn up on one of these pages. Just look around. I'm sure it was just here under the . . .

Hi, Snot Rag

(8-2)

As you can undoubtedly tell from the map (once you find it, that is), you've entered this maze facing the top of the I in the word COIN. You'll want to go south (yellow) until you reach the bottom of it.

The anagram directions, coupled with Eric Idle's interminably jolly bits of verbose encouragement, are fairly helpful. At the base of the I, trig hog. Ooops, that's "go right" (red arrow).

Follow Eric's urging on the next one, where your choice is straight on or to the right. Go straight on (red arrow).

At the three-way split in the track, go left (yellow

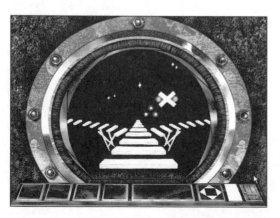

 Hello

arrow). At this point, you're exiting the word "coin" and heading into the word "slot." But, a brief warning — hang on to your seat! It's getting wavy, and oh, noooooooooo!

Whhhew. Well, it appears that the Inner Space car has landed safely on the word "slot," at the top of the letter L. Let's have a look around, shall we?

Go east (red arrow). This is the top of the S. Keep following the track around the curvaceous shape of the letter S until you hear the familiar whistling music. You're getting warmer!

Bravo. You've reached the trivia questions once again. The correct response to the first question appeared in the little ditty sung during the Money Programme. Do take that portrait offered and run along to the next one, and the next one, and so on until you've collected four portraits in Inner Space.

(Note: the portraits are randomly selected, so the ones that you are given may or may not correspond to those shown in the pictures illustrating this segment of the game. Now that that's all straightened out,

piss off and solve the rest of this lobe.)

You will probably want to record (either in your mind or on paper) the order of these portraits, which will be highly significant in the Portrait Gallery. In just a moment, that is.

THE PORTRAIT GALLERY

Now is that moment. Upon your return to the Portrait Gallery, go ahead and pick up that coin on the ground. That's right, go on, put it in the slot and see what happens. Now, pull the handle of the slot machine.

Your mission here is to choose the portraits that you found in the gallery in order, on the slots. It's as

simple as one, two, three...well, er, don't worry about the fourth one you've got, there. Yet.

Once the first three have been chosen correctly, the middle screen will begin to change horizontally. Choose your fourth portrait properly, and wait for the foot to drop!

Upon your triumphant return to the lobes of the brain, you'll notice that the Portrait Gallery lobe is now flashing merrily along with the other two. Good show! You've done it again!

So, off with you, then. Go play some more Spot the Looney!

SPOT THE LOONEY

Clues: Pneumatic Corridor. Hmmm. Around the Corridor, actually? Well, well.

Based upon these vague and utterly unintelligible clues, it is strongly suggested that you peep into the Corridor and find something useful to do there.

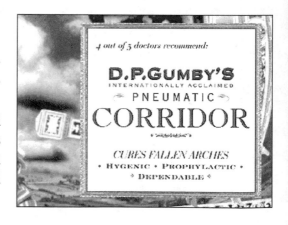

Mrs. Scum

SPLEEN 4

THE FINDINGS OF THE MINISTRY
OF SILLY KEYBOARD MANOEUVRES

Shift-Esc	Exits Complete Waste of Time
Esc	Takes you back to the Brain from any scene
Shift-B	Takes you directly to The Chicken Game
Shift-C	Takes you directly to the Corridor
Shift-D	Takes you directly to the Pythonizer
Shift-L	Takes you directly to the Loonatorium
Shift-G	Takes you directly to the Portrait Gallery
Shift-P	Takes you directly to The Pig Game
Shift-S	Takes you directly to the Stage
Shift-T	Takes you directly to the Exploding TV Room
Shift-W	Takes you directly to The Gopher Game
Shift-Z	Takes you directly to the Brain
Ctr-R	Toggles on/off restricted mode
Ctrl-S	Slows down the ball in the Pin Ball Game
Ctrl-F	Speeds up the ball in the Pin Ball Game

SPLEEN 5

YOUR WIFE, DOES SHE GO?

Norman: Is your wife a . . . goer . . . eh? Know what I mean? Know what I mean? Nudge nudge. Nudge nudge. Know what I mean? Say no more . . . know what I mean?

Him: I beg your pardon?

Norman: Your wife . . . does she, er, does she 'go' — eh? eh? eh? Know what I mean, know what I mean? Nudge nudge. Say no more.

Him: She sometimes goes, yes.

Norman: I bet she does. I bet she does. I bet she does. Know what I mean? Nudge nudge.

Him: I'm sorry, I don't quite follow you.

Norman: Follow me! Follow me! I like that. That's food. A nod's as good as a wink to a blind bat, eh? (elbow gesture, rubs it)

Him: Are you trying to sell something?

Norman: Selling, selling. Very good. Very good. Oh, wicked. Wicked. You're wicked. Eh? Know what I mean? Know what I mean? Nudge nudge. Know what I mean? Nudge nudge. Nudge nudge. Say . . . no . . . more.

Him: But . . .

Norman: Your wife is she, eh . . . is she a sport? Eh?

Him: She likes sport, yes.

Norman: I bet she does. I bet she does.

Him: She's very fond of cricket, as a matter of fact.

Norman: Who isn't, eh? Know what I mean? Likes games, likes games. Knew she would. Knew she would! Knew she would! She's been around, eh? Been around?

Him: She's travelled. She's from Purley.

Norman: Oh . . . oh. Say no more, say no more. Say no more, Purley, say no more. Purley, eh. Know what I mean, know what I mean? Say no more.

Him: (about to speak; can't think of anything to say)

Norman: Your wife interested in er . . . photographs, eh? Know what I mean? Photographs, 'he asked him knowingly'.

Him: Photography.

Norman: Yes. Nudge nudge. Snap snap. Grin, grin, wink, wink, say no more.

Him: Holiday snaps?

Norman: Could be, could be taken on holiday. Could be yes — swimming costumes. Know what I mean? Candid photography. Know what I mean, nudge nudge.

Him: No, no we don't have a camera.

Norman: Oh. Still Woah! Eh? Wo-oah! Eh?

Him: Look, are you insinuating something?

Norman: Oh . . . no . . . no . . . Yes.

Him: Well?

Norman: Well. I mean. Er, I mean. You're a man of the world, aren't you . . . I mean, er, you've er . . . you've been there haven't you . . . I mean you've been around . . . eh?

Him: What do you mean?

Norman: Well I mean like you've er . . . you've done it . . . I mean like, you know . . . you've . . . er . . . you've slept . . . with a lady.

Him: Yes.

Norman: What's it like?

SPLEEN G

DAMN AIR GAUGE → ANAGRAM GUIDE

GALLERY MAZE ANAGRAMS

Man as Rag → Anagrams

Let Ten Fix → Next Left

Texn Felt → Next Left

Duane Err at Thigh → Right Turn Ahead

Ah, Read Tight Um → Right Turn Ahead

Hi, Snot Rag → Straight On

Throng is Tar → Straight On

Or Thats Gin → Straight On

To Thin Rags → Straight On

Got Elf → Go Left

Felt Run → Left Turn

Furl Tent → Left Turn

Rent Flu There → Turn Left Here

Roth Gig → Go Right

Grog Hit → Go Right

Hog Grit → Go Right

Trig Hog → Go Right

Goth Rig → Go Right

Need Dad → Dead End

Bag OK, C? → Go Back

U Ran No Turd → Turn Around

Barber

SPLEEN 7

THE DIRTY VICAR

Dickie: Let us see the Dirty Vicar sketch.

Chivers: The Reverend Ronald Simms, the Dirty Vicar of St Michael's . . . ooh!

(Chivers is obviously goosed from behind by the Dirty Vicar.)

Vicar: Cor, what a lovely bit of stuff. I'd like to get my fingers around those knockers.

First Lady: How do you like the vicarage?

Vicar: I like tits!

First Lady: Oh vicar! vicar!

Vicar: Oh my goodness. I do beg your pardon. How dreadful! The first day in my new parist, I completely . . . so sorry!

First Lady: Yes. Never mind, never mind. Chivers — send Mary in with a new gown, will you?

Chivers: Certainly m'lady.

Vicar: (to the second lady) I do beg your pardon . . . I must sit down.

First Lady: As I was saying, how do you find the new vicarage?

Vicar: Oh yes, certainly, yes indeed, I find the grounds delightful, and the servants most attentive and particularly the little serving maid with the great big knockers . . . .

SPLEEN 8

INSERT COIN HERE

MONEY SONG

Presenter

I've got ninety thousand pounds in my pyjamas
I've got forty thousand French francs in my fridge.
I've got lots and lots of lira.
Now the Deutschmark's getting dearer.
And my dollar bills would buy the Brooklyn Bridge.

All

There is nothing quite as wonderful as money,
There is nothing quite as beautiful as cash,
Some people say it's folly
But I'd rather have the lolly
With money you can make a smash.

Presenter

There is nothing quite as wonderful as money
There is nothing like a newly minted pound

All

Everyone must hanker
For the butchness of a banker
It's accountancy that makes the world go round.

Presenter

You can keep your Marxist ways
For it's only just a phase.

All

For it's money, money, money
Makes the world go round.
Money, money, money, money, money, money!

NEXT CHAPTER: THE CORRIDOR

Many, many, many things fly around in this dazzling and unusual corridor, not the least of which are the colourful and not-too-enlightening Whizzo banners.

It must be noted that this Waste of Time becomes noticeably more difficult from this point on. The faint of heart may prefer simply to give up now and read a book, or engage in some other similarly productive activity.

Sigh…. Still here, are you? Well, consider yourself warned. Even the simple act of locating the Spanish Inquisitors is much, much trickier in the Corridor.

Oh, yes, and don't forget: If you need help, press F1.

The Whizzo Banners need to be furled before you can find the Inquisition. Fancy anyone actually WANTING to meet members of

38 TONS

10 (that's the number ten.)

the Spanish Inquisition. . . . The world's gone positively balmy. The trick is that there's an order to furling the banners. Start by clicking on the one on the left. Next, the yellow one in the middle. Third, the tippity-top one. Then, the one to the right. And finally, click on the little white Whizzo banner. There, that should do it.

The Spanish Inquisition

Now, you must turn off the pinball game by clicking on the green ON button in the top left corner.

As you run the cursor around the Corridor, you'll find the Spanish Inquisition door cleverly hidden behind the balcony far, far back in the Corridor. (It won't show up during the animations. You'll just have to wait.)

And before you can say Dinky Tinky—there you are, again, off to the mazes of Inner Space!

THE BANNER TRICK

1) Click on a banner.

Um. The one on the left. OK? Finished? On to the next step, then.

2) Now the yellow one. The one in the middle. In the middle.

3) Reach up now, to the very top banner. Click it. Right.

4) The one to the right.

5. That bitty little white Whizzo banner is last. Now it's time for pinball. Or maybe it's not. You figure it out. It's not my problem. What do you mean? It is not! Oh, bugger.

THE CORRIDOR MAZE

Warning: Dangerous, unpredictable maze!!!!

Ready to plunge on? Well, all right, then.

This is the maze that spells PIN BALL. There will be a series of lifts which take you from the word PIN to the B of BALL, and then a lift to each letter of the word BALL. Please pay close attention, and enjoy the ride.... No, don't.

Well, do.

No, don't.

Well, I insist, please do.

Bloody don't.

You begin (see map) at the lower right corner of the P, facing east (green arrow) to a dead end. Go ahead and turn left (blue arrow). And then left (red arrow) again. This takes you across the top of the P.

Ignore this sign!

At the top left corner of the P, go down (yellow arrow). Keep going down until you reach the dead end with a left turn. Follow Eric's cheery instruction; go left (green arrow).

Ignore this sign and turn left at the base of the I (blue arrow).

When you reach the top of the I, follow the sign about the lift. Except it isn't going down, now, is it? So, go on and take the lift up to the next level.

The lift. Down you go, then.
Or is it up?

Test Your Skill Maze *50*

Test Your Skill *53*

   The Gopher Game *53*

   The Pig Game *54*

   The Bird Game *55*

The Pythonizer *59*

   The Pythonizer Maze *59*

   The Pythonizer *66*

Back to the Brain *67*

Back to the Stage *68*

The Spleens

Spleen 1: The Argument Clinic *8*

Spleen 2: The Lumberjack Song *18*

Spleen 3: Exploding Penguin *25*

Spleen 4: Ministry of Silly Keyboard Manoeuvres *31*

Spleen 5: Your Wife, Does She Go? *32*

Spleen 6: Damn Air Gauge (Anagram Guide) *34*

Spleen 7: The Dirty Vicar *35*

Spleen 8: The Money Song *36*

Spleen 9: Dead Parrot *46*

Spleen 10: Cheese Shop *47*

Spleen 11: Room 12 . . . . *48*

Spleen 12: The Missing Map Page *58*

Spleen 13: Ridiculously Revealing Guide: Inner Space Questions *70*

Spleen 14: Ridiculously Revealing Guide: Spanish Inquisition Questions . . . *73*

Spleen 15: Test Your Skill Maze Anagrams *76*

Spleen 16: Inner Space Maps *77*

Spleen 17: The Llama *81*

NO TIME TO LOSE

TABLE OF CONTENTS

All that rubbish at the front of the book i
The Stuffy Forward vii
Vainglorious Acknowledgments vii

Monty Python: The Early Years . . . . Cancelled

The General Tips Part

The Lobes of the Brain 2
The Loonatorium 3
How to Bypass the Sketches 3
Access to Inner Space 4
Red Balls in the Air 4
Yellow Balls in the Air 5
The Trivia Questions 5
Shifting the Number of the Trivia Questions 5
The Reset Button 6
A good many extra words about this book 7

The Actual Book Part

The Loonatorium 10
   Finding Inner Space in the Loonatorium 12
   The Loonatorium Maze 13
   After Solving the Loonatorium Lobe 17

The Exploding TV Room 20
   The TV Maze 21
   Back to the Exploding TV Room 22

The Portrait Gallery 27
   Portrait Gallery Maze 28
   Back to the Portrait Gallery 29

The Corridor 37
   The Corridor Maze 39
   The Corridor (Revisited) 44
The Table of Contents 41
Test Your Skill 49

THE LETTER B

Don't be gullible. Ignore the signs.

You arrive at the top left corner of the letter B, facing down the left side (or south, if you prefer). Simply go straight down (yellow button) until you reach the bottom of the B. Ignore this sign, too. Make a left at the bottom of the B (green arrow) and take the lift that you find there.

Going down.

No, going up.

No, down.

I said, going up.

Just get on the bloody lift and go whichever direction it will take you! Up, perhaps.

THE LETTER A

You've taken the lift up, and now you've been deposited at the top left corner of the A. Your destination is the next lift at the bottom right leg of

The T track. Go right (yellow arrow).

the A. As you're facing south (down, or yellow arrow), make the first left (green arrow) to go across the A.

To get to the other side, of course.

Ignore all of the stupid, banal, irrelevant, argumentative signs that may cross your path. They're absolutely worthless. When you reach the T in the tracks, go right (yellow arrow). And of course, take the lift Up to the next level.

 Cannibalism

THE LETTER L (FIRST ONE)

As you're facing south (or yellow arrowly), you'll come to another lift or a left turn. Do NOT turn left. Merely take the lift Up to the next (and final) letter.

THE LETTER L (LAST ONE)

Lumberjack never wanted this job.

As you're facing south (or yellow arrowly), you'll come to another lift or a left turn. Do NOT take the lift, this time. Turn left (green arrow), and proceed to the end of the L. Oh, and, uh, pay attention to everything.

If you've gone all the way to the very end, bang up against the yellow stopper thingy with the number on it, and then back up from it. (Just click on the number to back up.) Once you reach the dead end at the bottom right of the L, you may have to wait a bit for something to happen. Really, you may have to wait for quite a long bit.

Hmmm, hmmm, hmmmm. Eventually, Eric will start humming, and then the questions will appear before your eyes.

As you defeat the maniacally difficult trivia questions devised by Them to confuse your feeble wits, you'll receive the usual assortment of essential clues. As these are generated totally at random (and thus will not conform to those appearing in this example), you may wish to write them down, in order, or otherwise notate them in some other way.

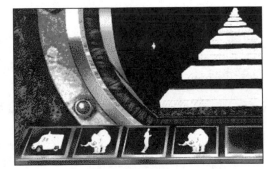

Don't be fooled.
Essential clues may vary.

No doubt the crosshairs have given you a hint (nudge, nudge, wink, wink, say — no — more!) about the fate of these symbols. In the pinball game, you know. OK, let's go.

THE CORRIDOR (REVISITED)

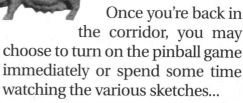

Flip the ball at the targets in the proper order and go waaaaah!

Once you're back in the corridor, you may choose to turn on the pinball game immediately or spend some time watching the various sketches...

Right. Now that you've turned the game on, it's time to spot your targets.

Pressing the down arrow key (on your keyboard) will get your ball in play, pushed off the ledge by the oinking piggy. The flippers can be controlled by the left and right arrows on your keyboard. (The ball can be slowed down by pressing Control + S.) Or, you can just use the mouse to shoot each target down.

Don't worry about hitting the targeted chickens; they're fair game but don't count for anything.

Major Hint:
Yes, you can hit the targets either by using the ball or, if you're really hopelessly lacking in motor skills, by clicking on them with the mouse.

Well, the idea (just between us, then) is that you must hit each of the Four Essential Clue targets in the order they've appeared in Inner Space. Remember, hit each one in the same order you got them in Inner Space, assuming you started with Question 1 and worked your way

3 or three

conventionally toward Question 4. Otherwise, look at the order of the targets in the control panel before you leave Inner Space. If you've forgotten the order, you can return to Inner Space to see them again.

Oh, and by the way, you must destroy all of your chosen targets, in order, using ONE ball.

Right. Good luck! (Hint: It's easier to fire on them with the mouse and crosshairs than to use the pinball flipper, especially if you have the misfortune to have John doing the Silly Walks as your target. Of course, that's not the truly butch way to go, but then nobody's looking. Are they?)

After you've hit all four of the targets, the pinball game will stop and a missile will splat onto the ground. Click on it, and out pops the foot that signifies the end of this lobe. You're free to go, now, you vacuous, toffee-nosed, malodorous pervert!

And you know where you're free to go next, don't you? Back to the Loonatorium, where looneys like you belong...!

The management would like to apologize for the unfortunate attitude displayed by the authors of this rather lengthy tome. It has come to our attention that they have been insulting our good readers, and we will have no more of it.

Sincerely,
The Management

SPLEEN 9

DEAD PARROT

Praline

Hello Polly, Polly (bangs it against counter) Polly Parrot, wake up. Polly. (throws it in the air and lets it fall to the floor) Now that's what I call a dead parrot.

Shopkeeper

No, no it's stunned.

Praline

Look, I took the liberty of examining that parrot, and I discovered that the only reason that it had been sitting on its perch in the first place was that it had been nailed there.

Shopkeeper

Well of course it was nailed there. Otherwise it would muscle up to those bars and voom.

Praline

Look matey (picks up parrot) this parrot wouldn't voom if I put four thousand volts through it. It's bleeding demised.

Shopkeeper

It's not, it's pining.

Praline

It's not pining, it's passed on. This parrot is no more. It has ceased to be. It's expired and gone to meet its maker. This is a late parrot. It's a stiff. Bereft of life, it rests in peace. If you hadn't nailed it to the perch, it would be pushing up the daisies. It's rung down the curtain and joined the choir invisible. This is an ex-parrot.

Superindendent Parrot

SPLEEN 10

CHEESE SHOP

Mousebender: Brie, Rocquefort, Pont-l'Evêque, Port Salut, Savoyard, Saint-Pulin, Carre-de-L'Est, Boursin, Bresse-Bleue, Perle de Champagne, Camembert?

Wensleydale: Ah! We do have some Camembert, sir.

Mousebender: You do. Excellent.

Wensleydale: It's a bit runny, sir.

Mousebender: Oh, I like it runny.

Wensleydale: Well as a matter of fact it's very runny, sir.

Mousebender: No matter. No matter. Hand over le fromage de la Belle France qui s'appelle Camembert, s'il vous plaît.

Wensleydale: I think it's runnier than you like it, sir.

Mousebender: (smiling grimly) I don't care how excrementally runny it is. Hand it over with all speed.

Wensleydale: Yes, sir. (bends below the counter and reappears) Oh. . .

Mousebender: What?

Wensleydale: The cat's eaten it.

Mousebender: Has he?

Wensleydale: She, sir.

Mousebender: It's not much of a cheese shop really, is it?

Wensleydale: Finest in the district, sir.

Mousebender: And what leads you to that conclusion?

Wensleydale: Well, it's so clean.

Mousebender: Well, it's certainly uncontaminated by cheese.

Wensleydale: You haven't asked me about Limberger, sir.

Mousebender: Is it worth it?

Wensleydale: Could be.

Mousebender: OK, have you . . . will you shut that bloody dancing up! (the music stops)

Wensleydale: (to dancers) Told you so.

SPLEEN 11

ROOM 12

Mr Barnard: (shouting) What do you want?

Man: Well I was told outside . . .

Mr Barnard: Don't give me that you snotty-faced heap of parrot droppings!

Man: What!

Mr Barnard: Shut your festering gob you tit! Your type makes me puke! You vacuous toffee-nosed malodorous pervert!!

Man: Look! I came in here for an argument.

Mr Barnard: (calmly) Oh! I'm sorry, this is abuse.

Man: Oh I see, that explains it.

Mr Barnard: No, you want room 12A next door.

Man: I see — sorry. (exits)

Mr Barnard: Not at all. (as he goes) Stupid git.

THE LOONATORIUM

A handful of unintelligible sound effects and the "Whack a Mole—Try The Gopher Game" visual clue... perhaps it's time to visit the Test-Your-Skill lobe. Since it's time to try The Gopher Game, click on the little Victorian woman symbol in the bottom left of the lobe.

5 or five

MORONIC CHAPTER: TEST YOUR SKILL

Are you a man or a doorstop? Time to separate the camembert from the stilton. You've got three choices in Test Your Skill, but unless you slept through the previous page, you've likely figured out the clue. So grab your mallet and whack off. Go right ahead.

THE GOPHER GAME

Go ahead and play the game for a bit. Eventually, the doorway to the Spanish Inquisition sketch (and Inner Space) will pop up, remarkably enough like a gopher, from one of the holes.

THE TEST YOUR SKILL MAZE

Test Your Skill Maze

Test Your Skill Maze Map: Start at the O and get to the X.

This is the maze that spells WHACK A MOLE. You enter at the left base of the first letter A. Turn around (blue arrow) and go up, then make a right (green arrow) to cross the A. Go right (yellow arrow) and down, to reach the base of the right leg of the A. Next, go left (green arrow) to reach the letter C.

Now pay attention. It is important that these directions be followed precisely: Turn left (blue arrow) to go up the C. Once you reach the top of the C, do not go across it! Just turn around (yellow arrow) and go back down to the base of the C. You'll see a T in the track — and the lift!

Take the lift going down to the next word, A. And the next letter, A. After all, they're one and the same.

You enter the A at the bottom of the right leg. Just go ahead and go up, or north, or the blue arrow direction. Follow the sign, and listen to Eric. U ran no turd!!! Oh, that's turn around! (Yellow button, then.)

You'll come upon a track veering off from the right. Ignore it, and go straight on.

Ignore this sign, too, OK? Just take the lift going down.

Finally, you arrive at the base (left) of the letter M in MOLE. Go ahead and let the game run you to the top of the M, then go right (green arrow) to cross the top left side. Your ultimate destination is the top right bar of the letter E.

The quickest way to get there from here:

- Right across top of M, left side (green arrow)
- Right down left middle piece of M (yellow arrow)
- Left across middle of M (green arrow)
- Left up the right middle piece of M (blue arrow)
- Right across top of M, right side (green arrow)

Don't go across the top of the C. Turn around and go back to this **T**.

Ignore this track and the sign (above). Just go on and take the lift down to the letter **M**.

- Right down right side of M (yellow arrow)
- Left at base of M, connecting to O (green arrow)
- Straight across bottom of O and L (green arrow three times)

Note: If the "car" stops, keep pressing the green arrow until it's moving again.

- Left up spine of letter E (blue arrow)
- Straight up spine of E (blue arrow)
- Right across top of E (green arrow)

All right, now all you need to do is press the button. Really.

And answer all of the questions.

(Note: The numbers of the essential clues are randomly generated, so your numbers may or may not match those depicted in the illustrations in this guide. If this situation does not meet with your approval, you may just bugger off.

Your Four Essential Clues may vary.
Don't be fooled by cheap imitations.

> We've already had a word about the level of verbal abuse on the part of our authors, haven't we? Hmmmmmm?
> **The Management**

Time to exit Inner Space and go back into the Test Your Skill lobe.

TEST YOUR SKILL

Now then, for those of you still engaged in this Complete Waste of Time, the clues tell you that The Gopher Game is to be played first.

The numeric clues are the scores you are to achieve playing each separate Test Your Skill game. The trick is, in what order do you play them? If you've strayed from the directions in this maze, you've probably collected the non-essential clues, which give you broad hints about the necessary order of play.

If you haven't collected any of those, you're really out of luck, aren't you!? Oh, all RIGHT. The order of the games is as follows:

1. Furry, yard-ripping rodent game
2. Hoary mud-wallowing mammal game
3. Avian creature on its way to join the Choir Invisible game

In other words, The Gopher Game, The Pig Game, The Bird Game. Happy now?

THE GOPHER GAME

(In the example shown, the player must achieve 25 points to "win" The Gopher Game. As this number was randomly chosen in Inner Space, yours will probably differ as you approach these Test Your Skill games. Use the first set of digits you received in The Gopher Game.)

- There is a time limit, so play carefully!
- Each head whacked gains you one point.
- Each miss loses one point.
- Each bobby you whack gains you five points.

54 TONS Monty Python's Complete Waste of Time, Etc. . . .

- Whacks on flying chicken in the air win 10 points.
- Whacks on the tuxedoed bloke with wings win five points.
- Whacks on the flying valkyrie win seven or eight points, but no one's quite certain about the total.
- Whacking the Whack Lady (yes, you can make her whack herself) loses 15 points.

Good luck!

Once you've managed to reach your first desired score in The Gopher Game, it will send you back out to the lobes. Check under the Test Your Skill to make sure that The Gopher Game icon (the Victorian miss) is lit up and flashing merrily. Right. Now, it's on to The Pig Game.

THE PIG GAME

Hit the enter button to begin the game. The idea here is to shoot at the giant pig in the sky, using the directional arrow keys on your keyboard, before it can squeeze out a repulsive turd which will then turn into a small but vicious piglet who will kill you doornail dead. You get a certain number of points for shooting the little piggies that break off of the giant pig.

Happy shootin'!

(In the example given, the player needs to attain 10 points in The Pig Game in order to move on to the third and final one. In your case, use the second set of digits received in Inner Space.)

Once you've completed The Pig Game, you'll return to the lobes and should observe the pig icon and the Victorian lady from The Gopher Game flashing. On to the third Test Your Skill Game: The Bird Game.

Death by pig excrement. Don't let this fate befall you!

THE ~~CHICKEN~~ BIRD GAME

THE STRATEGY TO PLAYING THE BIRD GAME

- ⇢ Wait until the gaping mouth on the left is on its way up, about a quarter of the way open.

- ⇢ Immediately press the Enter key at that point, then wait until the Chicken Man falls from his perch to a position just below the electrical shocker doohickey.

- ⇢ Then quickly and repeatedly press the left arrow on the keyboard. Don't press anything else. Keep pressing until the Chicken Man hits the eating man.

If your timing is exact, the Chicken Man will be guided safely into the mouth. Otherwise, he'll be munched in half, his little body will fly off into two separate parts and you'll lose a point in the process.

6 or six

Click on the head on the ledge to the right of the screen. It will hatch into one of those obnoxious chickens you've been shooting at, all game long. The idea is to guide the chicken success- fully into the gaping mouth on the left of the screen, using the direction arrows on the keyboard. At all costs, avoid hitting the spikes on the bottom (and don't let them hit your chicken, either!) and the electric shocker at the top of the screen.

- Spikes cost two points
- Electric chicken bake costs two points
- Missing the mouth and getting eaten costs one point
- In the mouth gains five points

There's a golden place at the open mouth where the chicken just sails right in. This is a matter of pacing the cracking of the head and navigating the chicken at just the right time.

The golden spot.

When you've defeated The Bird Game and gotten the entire Test Your Skill Lobe blinking, you know there's only one place left to visit; the Loonatorium. Must get those clues before you go rushing into the Pythonizer, y'know.

Whizzo

THE LOONATORIUM

Your clues: Don't accessorize, Pythonize! Explore the Pythonizer... and the Larch...the Larch. (The Larch ????!?!)

So, it's off to the Pythonizer with you, you stupid git. As you get clos- er and closer to the Secret of Success, don't lose your head!

SPLEEN 12

THE MISSING MAP PAGE

Gallery Maze

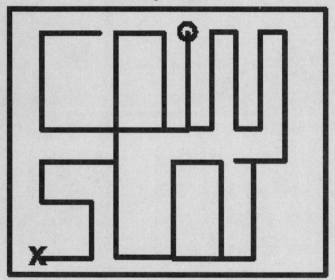

Corridor Maze

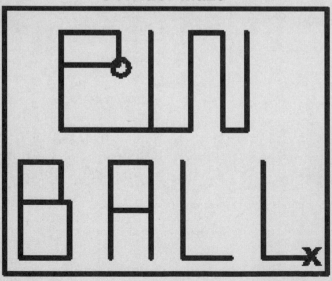

We found the maps! OK. So they're a bit late. We realize that some of you have been lost for some time now, and our hearts are bleedin'. Honest. Please cease your snivelling — immediately — and take note of these page numbers:

The Gallery Maze description can be found on page 28.

The Corridor Maze description can be found on page 39.

Now, if you're satisfied, we'll get on with the book. That is, if you've got no other questions. Nothing to say? Right, then. On with the book.

THE LAST CHAPTER: THE PYTHONIZER

The door into Inner Space is located on the lower left side of the screen. Go ahead and click on the screen somewhere to trigger the start of the Pythonizer music. Once the hand begins to turn on the grinder, the door will be lurking near the bottom of the screen.

Pythonizer Maze

Ronald Simms

Well, it certainly starts off with a bang, hey?

As you end up under water, just suffer through all of the clever Pythonizer animations and so on. Oh, and do press the Space Bar when needed.

You'll face the button at the end of the track. This is the maze that spells MEAT HEAD GRINDER, and you're facing the base of the M, my friend. The veritable bottom of the heap, if you get the drift.

The first thing to do is to turn yourself around (with the blue arrow) and go north, or up (if you must), the left side of the M. Your destination is the top left side of the top of the T.

Here are the quick directions to get you there:

(If you haven't done so already, up the left leg of the M, using the blue arrow.) Oh, yes, and be sure to ignore the abominably unhelpful and thoroughly useless signs, won't you?

- Right across the top of M, left side (green arrow)
- Right down left middle piece of M (yellow arrow)
- Left across middle of M (green arrow)
- Left up right middle piece of M (blue arrow)
- Right across top of M, right side (green arrow)
- Right down right side of M (yellow arrow)
- Left across connecting track to letter E (green arrow)
- Straight across base of E (green arrow)
- Left up left side of A (blue arrow)
- Right at first fork of A, across the middle of A (green arrow)
- Right at right side of A, going down the right side of A (yellow arrow)
- Left to connect to letter T (green arrow)
- Left at base of T, going up T (blue arrow)
- Left at top of T (in fact, the T at the top of the T!) (red arrow)
- Take the lift going down to the word HEAD
- You arrive at the top right bar of the letter E, facing the top left corner. Make a left (yellow arrow) to go down the back of the E.

2 (the number two)

- Straight ahead at the left track, down the E (yellow arrow again)
- Left at the T, across the base of the E and up to the A (green arrow)
- Left to go up left leg of A (blue arrow)
- Right across middle of A (green arrow)
- Right down right leg of A (yellow arrow)
- Left connecting to D (green arrow)
- Straight ahead, past left side of D (green arrow)
- Left up bottom right link of D (blue arrow)
- Turn around (yellow arrow)
- Take the lift down to the word GRINDER

Sign on the left side of the D.

Danger!

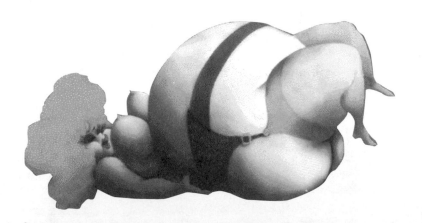

It's a bit of a rocky ride down to the GRINDER, but don't let it shake you up. You arrive at the very inside of the letter G (see map), facing up. Your goal is to reach the bottom of the very far right leg of the very far right letter R. The path that lies ahead, between the innocent G and the dastardly RINDER, is treacherous at best. Well, you didn't seriously think they'd ease up on you, now, did you? Pay close attention to the deja vu music in the letters R. . . .

Press on, then!

- Right along top of tail of letter G (green arrow)
- Right down right side of letter G (yellow arrow)
- Left at T in the tracks to connect to letter R (green arrow)
- Left up left side of letter R (blue arrow)

When you see this bit of track, with the right one intersecting at an angle, and hear the deja vu sequence from "It's the Mind," you know you're in trouble. (See sidebar below.)

An interesting bit of track.

In fact, They (the devious designers of this so-called game) want you to be in real trouble, to go around and around in the top loops of the letter R, stuck for days on end with no hope of survival. (They're really a lot more nefarious than you may think from Their harmless exteriors, you know.) Once you're caught in the infamous "Deja Vu Death Loop", you'll forget to eat, to sleep, and to move. A veritable statue of yourself, ultimately your body will just waste away as you moan quietly, "Oh, God, not this section of track AGAIN!" Then They'll come into your house and make off with all of your most valuable possessions — the dead parrot, the exploded telly, and the pinball machine, just to name a few of your favourites. Ah, but there is a way out. Honest. Just turn the page!

NO TIME
TO LOSE

THE TECHNIQUE FOR THE LETTERS R IN "GRINDER"

Fortunately, there are ways around the horrendous "Deja Vu Death Loop" that will allow you to retain your sanity (though why you'd want it is beyond Us) as well as your most valuable possessions.

Once you've reached that peculiar piece of track (previous page), go straight on, one link ahead (blue arrow). (Ignore the button ahead of you.). Then, right across the top of the R (green arrow),

At this bizarre intersection, go right across inner bar of R (red arrow).

and turn right, down the top side of the R (yellow).

When you reach the bizarre intersection (above), go right across the inner bar of the R (red arrow). You'll come to this same bizarre diagonal "T" intersection again. Turn around! (green arrow) Keep going straight (green arrow) no matter what! (This is the part that takes you out of the dreaded "Deja Vu Death Loop".)

- After escaping the "Death Loop," go right, down the right leg of the letter R (yellow arrow).
- Left at the connecting track between the R and the I (green arrow).
- Although it appears that you've reached a dead end, pay no attention.
- Just make a left, up the I (blue arrow).
- When the car stops, just keep clicking on the arrow until it moves again.
- Ignore the button at the top of the I, and turn around (yellow arrow).

65 TONS

- This time when you reach the bottom of the I, you will be presented with a T intersection in the track.
- Go left along the track that connects to the letter N (green arrow).
- Left up the side of the N (blue arrow).

- Right across the left-most top of the N (green arrow).
- Right down the middle of the N (yellow arrow).
- Left across the bottom of the N (green arrow).
- The right side of the N functions like the I. Make a left to go up (blue arrow), then turn around and find the T intersection that allows you to continue on to the letter D (yellow arrow).
- Make a left at another T intersection (green arrow).
- Oh yes, and do ignore Eric's taunting.
- Straight ahead past the left side of the D (green arrow).
- And straight ahead again past the right side of it (green arrow).
- And straight ahead again past the spine of the E (green arrow).
- Make a right at the base of the R (blue arrow).
- Go straight ahead (blue arrow) and follow the steps mentioned on the other R to avoid the dreaded Deja Vu Death Loop.
- Right (green arrow).
- Right (yellow arrow).
- Right (red arrow).
- Turn around (green arrow).
- Straight on (green arrow).
- Right to go down leg of R (yellow arrow).

And then, the questions!!!!!

And remember, Nobody likes a Benedict!

Dead

Got all of your visual clues? Remember them in order of appearance? Great.

Let's go back to the Pythonizer. One. . . last. . . time.

THE PYTHONIZER

As you click on the grinder, the faces of those clues you've just worked so hard to win will pop up. Choose each face in its proper sequence, and drag it into the grinder (just below the hand). (It's kind of a more ghoulishly satisfying Spot the Looney.)

Really. That's all there is to it!

BACK TO THE BRAIN

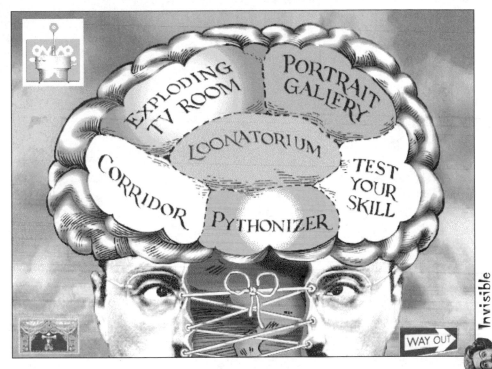

Once you've finished in The Pythonizer, you will return to the lobes and be gratified to see them all winkly and twinkly, lit up like cheesy little Christmas lights. Congratulations! You've done it! You've won it! You've...you've completed the devious Python brain!

Well, almost.

See that icon in the upper left corner? The one that wasn't there before?

When you click on it, the Devious Python Brain will become a game of Simon. Remember Simon? That grotty little game that beeped and urped obnoxious colour patterns at you that you had to mimic, feeling utterly ridiculous as you did so?

Indeed. The same principle is at work, here. Follow the first three sets of patterns by clicking on the appropriate lobes of the brain.

And don't worry when it gets impossibly fast. All you need do is tap the correct number of lobes, not follow the colours at all. Got that?

When the game gets really, really fast so that Colin Mozart himself wouldn't be able to keep up, just tap the mouse button the correct number of times without regard for the actual lobes themselves. That's all you need to do. Tap the button on any lobe — or combination of lobes. Come to think of it, you've done little more than that since you began this ridiculous Waste Of Time.

BACK TO THE STAGE

Ah...Deja Vu. We've been here before, way back when we first started this whole exercise in futility and foolishness. Back to the stage. Stage one, you might say...hmm, yes. Here you'll dodder through a remarkable congratulations ceremony. A sketch will begin, one about replacing the old brain with a new one...and then you will finally, ultimately, in the end, after all, at last, at long last, conclusively, decisively, absolutely, definitely, once and for all discover the Secret to Intergalactic Success!!!

Which is...

(Imagine a sixteen-ton weight landing firmly on the craniums of the authors of this remark- ably astute and well-  that self-same weight falling on your own head.... No, seriously, if you honestly thought that we were going to written booklet that you're cur- rently holding in your hot, grub- by little hands. In fact, imagine tell you the answer, you have a pressing need to join Mrs. Scum for more blows on the head....)

a head

70
TONS

SPLEEN 10

THE RIDICULOUSLY REVEALING GUIDE TO THE TRIVIA QUESTIONS

INNER SPACE QUESTIONS

 Look for me!

THE LOONATORIUM MAZE

Question #1: What is the first word said in Storytime?
Answer: See page 28

Question #2: The mountain with the biggest tits in the world
Answer: See page 22

Question #3: Colour of telephone in Argument Clinic
Answer: See page 39

Question #4: Who ate the Crunchy Frog?
Answer: See page 46

THE EXPLODING TV ROOM MAZE

Question #1: What currency is kept in the fridge?
Answer: See page 27

Question #2: Ant body sections.
Answer: See page 44

Question #3: Number of times the Parrot is beaten against the
counter
Answer: See page 48

Question #4: Number of unsuccessful encyclopedia sales-
men
Answer: See page 44

ZOP

THE PORTRAIT GALLERY MAZE

Question #1: What currency is kept in the pyjamas?
Answer: See page 75

Question #2: Who opts for the Blow on the Head?
Answer: See page 30

Question #3: Parrot joined this choir.
Answer: See page 67

to lose

Question #4: First lesson of not being seen is not to . . .
Answer: See page 52

THE CORRIDOR MAZE

Question #1: Flying banner brand name.
Answer: See page 57

Question #2: Lumberjack never wanted this job.
Answer: See page 34

Question #3: Dirty Vicar's real name.
Answer: See page 59

Question #4: They can be recognized from a really long way away.
Answer: See page 16

THE TEST YOUR SKILL MAZE

Question #1: How many years until Ken Shabby gets a brush?
Answer: See page 48

Question #2: Atilla the Hun's gift to children.
Answer: See page 69

Question #3: What room is the Argument Clinic in?
Answer: See page 17

Question #4: Number of cars at drive-in.
Answer: See page 56

THE PYTHONIZER MAZE

Question #1: What is an alternative to burning, burying or dumping?
Answer: See page 77

Question #2: What is the full-time occupation for the cat influenza man?
Answer: See page 23

Question #3: Nobody likes a . . .
Answer: See page 81

Question #4: How many seconds of sex?
Answer: See page 38

Beautiful plumage

SPLEEN 11

RIDICULOUSLY REVEALING GUIDE TO MORE TRIVIA QUESTIONS

Spanish Inquisition Questions

Complete the following phrase: Spanish . . .

see page 79

Complete the following phrase: Ee Eecky . . .

see page 21

Complete the following phrase: Hold your head and go . . .

see page 28

Complete the following phrase: Hello, . . .

see page 13

Complete the following phrase: The man with three . . .

see page 49

Complete the following phrase: Old Nick the . . .

see page 78

What did Rumpletweezer run?

see page 19

What does the Norwegian Blue have?

see page 72

Complete the following phrase: No time . . .

see page 71

Complete the following phrase: Spam, bacon, sausage and . . .

see page 60

How many verses are there in the Lumberjack song?

see page 45

How many lobes of the Brain are there?

see page 56

How many Mounties sing the chorus?

see page 8

How many blows on the head does Mrs. Scum receive?

see page 24

How many people are watching television?

see page 24

How many Spanish Inquisitors were there?

see page 44

How many Can Can girls are there?

see page 61

How many explosions are there in the Exploding Blue Danube?

see page 25

In what room is the Argument Clinic?

see page 17

What color is the door in the Argument Clinic?

see page 2

How does Polly parrot feel?

see page 65

Complete the following phrase: Your wife, is she a . . .

see page 50

Who did the Lumberjack want by his side?

see page 18

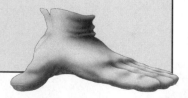

What breed is the killer cat?

see page 80

Complete the following phrase: I say, anyone for . . .

see page 26

Complete the following phrase: You make me want to . . .

my guts out.

see page 11

Complete the following phrase: Sorry, Squire, I . . . on your carpet.

see page 66

What problem does the Royal Navy have under control?

see page 42

How many hours does it take to bury the cat?

see page 45

An ant battling a wolf takes up to how long?

see page 54

Which cheese was eaten by the cat?

see page 14

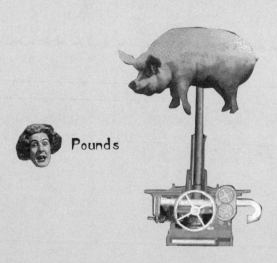

Pounds

SPLEEN 13

TEST YOUR SKILL MAZE ANAGRAMS

Let Ten Fix → Next Left

Elf N Text → Next Left

Hi, Snot Rag → Straight On

To Thin Rags → Straight On

Let Fog → Go Left

Got Elf → Go Left

Oft Leg → Go Left

Felt Runt → Left Turn

Then Leaf a Turd → Left Turn Ahead

Ouch Not d'Tit → Don't Touch It

SPLEEN 14

THE INNER SPACE MAPS

Loonatorium Maze

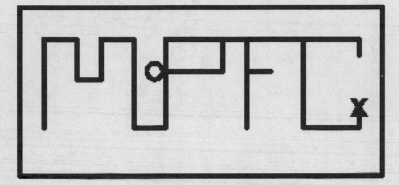

TV Room Maze

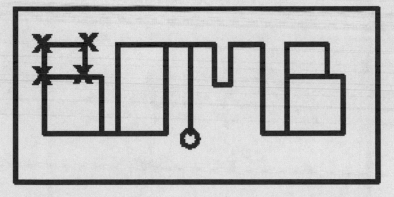

Eating

Gallery Maze

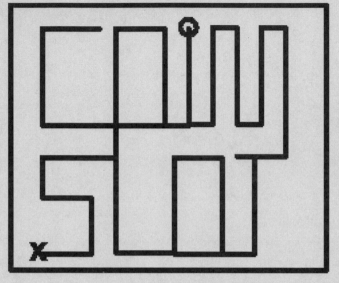

Corridor Maze

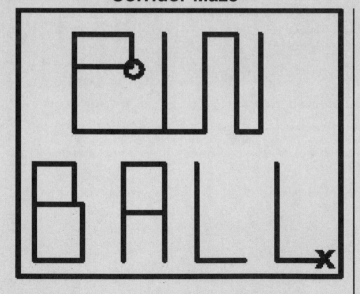

 Sea Captain

Test Your Skill Maze

Inquisition

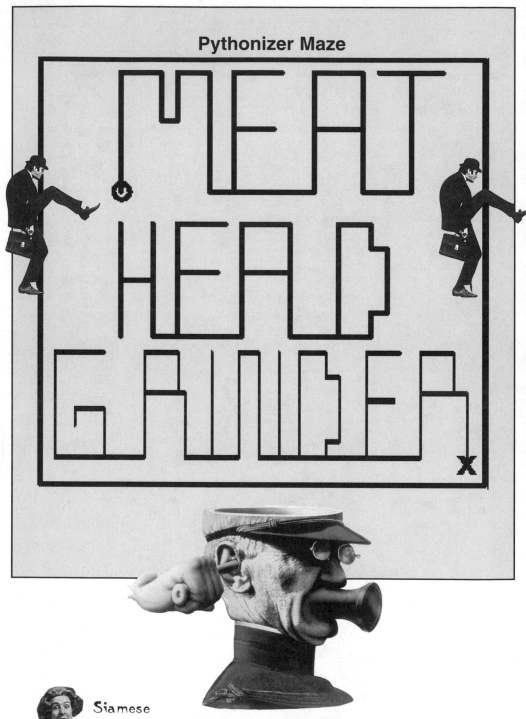

Pythonizer Maze

SPLEEN 15

THE LLAMA

Man enters and walks up to a life-size photo of a llama. He delivers the following lecture in Spanish, with help from the guitarist and dancer, and superimposed subtitles.

Man: (but in Spanish with subtitles in English) The llama is a quadruped which lives in big rivers like the Amazon. It has two ears, a heart, a forehead, and a beak for eating honey. But it is provided with fins for swimming.

Guitarist & Dancer: Llamas are larger than frogs.

Man: Llamas are dangerous, so if you see one where people are swimming, you shout:

Guitarist & Dancer: Look out, there are llamas!

Benedict

82 TONS

SOLVE THE SECRET TO INTERGALACTIC **Success**

MONTY PYTHON'S

COMPLETE WASTE OF TIME